The Majesty of the Felicianas

The Majesty of the

FELICIANAS

Photography by Paul Malone
Text by Lee Malone

PELICAN PUBLISHING COMPANY

GRETNA 1989

Malone, Paul.
   The majesty of the Felicianas / photography by Paul Malone ; text
by Lee Malone.
      p.   cm.
   ISBN 0-88289-712-8
   1. Plantations—Louisiana—East Feliciana Parish—Pictorial works.
   2. Plantations—Louisiana—West Feliciana Parish—Pictorial works.
   3. East Feliciana Parish (La.)—Description and travel—Views.
   4. West Feliciana Parish (La.)—Description and travel—Views.
   I. Malone, Lee. II. Title.
   F377.E3M35 1989
   779'.9976316—dc19   88-29072
                                                                  CIP

Photo on p. 2: Above Parlange's hand-carved cypress mantelpiece is a French beveled mirror in a gold-leaf frame with pierced carving on top. Note the bronze Doré clock on the mantel and the bronze statue of Esmerelda to the side of the mantel.

Photo on p. 6: Spiraling from the ground floor to the upper levels of Ellerslie, the staircase is an engineering marvel.

Photo on p. 8: Above the carved-cypress mantelpiece at Oakley hangs an original Audubon painting. The mahogany punkah above the table and chairs was moved back and forth to fan the diners. Next to the fireplace stands an antique plate warmer.

Photo on p. 10: An elaborate etagere stands in the upstairs hall at Milbank, displaying antique china, figurines, and an unusual clock.

Book design by Dana Bilbray

Printed in Singapore through Palace Press
Published by Pelican Publishing Company, Inc.
1101 Monroe Street, Gretna, Louisiana 70053

To the plantation home owners and curators
who welcomed us and shared the joy
that dwells within these beautiful old homes.

Acknowledgments

Michael M. Pilié, for his perceptive encouragement.

Carl L. LeBoeuf II, laboratory technician, for his printing expertise and dedication throughout the compiling of this book.

David Floyd, site manager, Louisiana State Department of Parks, for his assistance and enthusiasm.

Mary Ellen Young of the West Feliciana Historical Society, for her assistance in gathering information on several of the plantations.

Jim Calhoun, Dr. Milburn Calhoun, Nancy Calhoun, and their staff, for their proficiency and guidance.

Contents

Introduction

In the early 1700s a group of French settlers were attracted to the long ridge located in the center of what is today West Feliciana Parish. The settlement they founded was called the Village of St. Francis in honor of St. Francis of Assisi, founder of the Franciscan Order. As the town grew, it became known as St. Francisville.

The area surrounding St. Francisville consists of East and West Feliciana parishes. These are the most verdantly beautiful parishes in Louisiana, partially because the soil was enriched for centuries by fine-grained, fertile loam deposited by transcontinental winds from glacial deposits and river deltas to the banks of the Mississippi River. Lush shrubbery and colorful blooms abound there in all seasons of the year, and countless birds nest in the trees of the fragrant woodlands.

Picturesque bayous, small rivers, and streams are interspersed throughout the Felicianas, and along the banks of the waterways vast, productive plantations were established. As the plantations prospered, grand homes were built by the owners, who became widely known for their elaborate showplaces and enchanting gardens.

For many years before the Civil War, the planters and their families enjoyed prosperity. They visited each other's homes for elegant dinner parties at which fine cuisine, including tropical fruits, were served. They also attended horse racing, which was the most exciting sport. A racing season took place at St. Francisville as early as March 1, 1831. Trips to New Orleans and to other parts of the world provided further pleasant diversion.

All of this came to an abrupt halt with the outbreak of the Civil War. Many of the planters immediately joined the Confederate Army. Their families, so unfamiliar with adversity, assumed the responsibility of managing plantation affairs. Many families rose to the challenge and faced with courage the burning of their homes, the confiscation of their food and crops, and numerous other indignities inflicted by Federal troops.

When the Civil War ended, the Confederate forces returned home to find bleak devastation. Many of the glorious mansions had been destroyed by fire, and many of them had been severely damaged. During the years of Reconstruction, the scorched earth and the lack of money caused some of the once-prosperous plantations to be abandoned. The homes that were left to the elements further deteriorated.

Numerous fortunes had been rebuilt by the 1940s and 1950s. Restoration of the timeworn homes began about that time, and many of those residences now stand proudly in their original glory. Thus, the majesty of the Felicianas has returned in all its splendor.

The Majesty of the Felicianas

Afton Villa Gardens
St. Francisville

Afton Villa began with the Barrows and was owned and loved throughout the years by a succession of families, all of whom contributed to its strange, haunting beauty.

In 1790 Bartholomew Barrow bought the large tract of land, part of a Spanish land grant on which an early-type, eight-room house stood. After Bartholomew's death, his son David lived there with his bride, Sarah, until she died in childbirth in 1846.

A year later, David married Susan Woolfolk of Kentucky, and it was she who desired a more pretentious dwelling. Construction of the larger Afton Villa began in 1849 and lasted for eight years. David had given his wife one restriction: that the original house, for sentimental reasons, would remain intact. The new mansion therefore was built around the small cottage.

A French architect was commissioned to come to St. Francisville to supervise the work. When completed, Afton Villa was a magnificent forty-room manor of French-Gothic architecture.

After David's death, the villa changed ownership several times until it was purchased in 1945 by Mr. and Mrs. Wallace Percy. The Percys restored the house to its original splendor, only to see it destroyed by fire in 1963.

The gardens of Afton Villa were planned originally by a French landscape gardener. To the left of the ruins of the house are stone steps leading into a delightful formal boxwood garden, laid out as an intricate maze. Colorful camellias, sweet olive, fuscata, azaleas, and flowering bulbs bloom there

profusely. Immediately below the formal garden is a large sweep of seven graded terraces that descend to the ravine. Each terrace is ablaze with vivid flowers.

Another interesting, though hidden, feature of the gardens is the network of French drains which underlies the surface of the park. The system, constructed of brick, still functions, thus preventing erosion of the rolling slopes.

Between the rows of hedges, Red Diplomat, Smiling Queen, and Maureen tulips are underplanted with mixed pansies.

White tulips, begonias, and blue pansies add to the beauty of Afton Villa Gardens.

In the garden behind the Afton Villa ruins are Golden Oxford tulips and Louisiana phlox underplanted with yellow pansies.

Impressive statues guard the entrance to the main gardens at Afton Villa. Note the Golden Oxford tulips.

The statue seems to be contemplating the serenity of the scene at Afton Villa Gardens created by moss-draped live oak trees.

An antique bed of simple but elegant design stands in this Barrow House bedroom. The Empire round table dates from the 1840s. The armoire has pierced carving on top and two mirrored doors.

This Barrow House bedroom view shows the beautiful satin lining of the full-tester bed. The Empire marble-topped bureau, with mirror and wishbone design, was made about 1840.

The mahogany punkah shown here was moved back and forth by servants for the comfort of the diners. The mahogany Empire table and chairs, ca. 1850, and the old crystal candelabra in the center of the table add to the attractiveness of the room.

18

Camilla Leake Barrow House

St. Francisville

On historic tree-shaded Royal Street in the town of St. Francisville, Camilla Leake Barrow House stands with quiet dignity. It was built in 1809 by the town jailer, Daniel J. Manire, as a "salt box" structure consisting of two rooms on each of the two levels.

The home changed hands several times before 1858 when J. Hunter Collins bought the quaint cottage. He also bought a small cottage on an adjoining lot and had it moved so that it could be attached to the original structure of Barrow House. He then added beautiful cast-ironwork railings to the upper and lower galleries, giving the house its present stately appearance.

Above the antique console table hangs a charcoal drawing of the original Camilla Leake Barrow House.

In 1866 W. W. Leake purchased the property, and it remained in his family's possession for 125 years. In 1895, Leake's daughter, Camilla, inherited the house and then married Dr. A. F. Barrow of Greenwood. Since that time it has been known as the Camilla Leake Barrow House.

Lyle and Shirley Dittloff began a new era by purchasing the beautiful old home in 1984. It is listed in the National Register of Historic Places.

The marble mantelpiece and the gold-leaf framed mirror above it command attention in this parlor at Asphodel.

Below: Sliding doors separate the double parlors at Asphodel. Identical antique furniture is found in each parlor.

A beautiful chandelier hangs above the mahogany dining room table at Asphodel. The sideboard is by Prudent Mallard.

Asphodel

Near Baton Rouge

Ten years were required to construct the huge stone structure of Asphodel. Benjamin Kendrick, the builder, died in 1830, the year the home was completed, and his daughter, Isobel Kendrick Fluker, inherited the house. Though she had been an only child, she and her husband had twelve children. From that time until the Civil War, Asphodel rang with the voices and laughter of a happy family.

Isobel's husband died before the Civil War; therefore, only she and her children met the Union troops who came to Asphodel in search of food. During one raid the members of the family locked themselves in the library and hid in fear while the troops set the house afire. Because so little wood had been used in the construction of the house, the fire was soon extinguished.

The Flukers faced many impoverished years after the war, and the home eventually came into the possession of the Misses Smith, who also were descendants of the original owners. They lived at Asphodel for forty years.

In 1949 the John Fetzers bought and restored this beautiful plantation house. After Fetzer's death, Asphodel was sold to the present owner, Robert E. Couhig, in 1959.

Bonnie Burn
Clinton

Amid beautifully landscaped grounds, Bonnie Burn stands in stately splendor. It was built shortly after Elisha and Martha Hamlin purchased the land in September of 1857.

During the Civil War, a detachment of Confederate soldiers, under the command of Col. Fred Ogden, engaged in a skirmish nearby with Union troops. In the course of the fight Bonnie Burn, then known as the Hamlin Place, was fired upon and sustained damage. A Minié ball fired by a Union soldier passed through a south window of the house and through the wall of the downstairs hallway.

This burled walnut bed at Bonnie Burn was made by New Orleans cabinet-makers Barnes and McCracken.

J. G. Kilbourne, great-grandfather of the present owner, Richard Holcombe Kilbourne, bought the home in 1868. J. G. Kilbourne had graduated from Centenary College in Jackson, Louisiana, on July 31, 1850, and became a prominent attorney. When the Civil War erupted, he joined the Hunter Rifles, which was composed of 153 men from Clinton and the surrounding area. The group left the town on April 30, 1861, and eventually

became a part of the Fourth Louisiana Infantry Regiment. After the war Kilbourne practiced law in Clinton. During the years of Reconstruction he played a notable role in helping to deliver East Feliciana Parish from the domination of carpetbaggers and scalawags.

Bonnie Burn means *pretty creek*, and this name was bestowed upon a nearby stream by J. G. Kilbourne's youngest daughter, Margaret. The lovely home also became known by the same name.

In Greek Revival style, impressive pillars dominate the façade of the house. The high-pitched roof is broken by dormer windows. The gallery extends across the front of the structure, and the second story features a balcony above the front entrance doorway. The balustrade is of intricate iron filigree.

Descendants of J. G. Kilbourne occupy and maintain this magnificent home.

Note the sturdiness of the staircase in the entrance hallway at Bonnie Burn. An old Dutch chandelier lights the hallway where two antique bookcases stand against the wall.

The parlor at Bonnie Burn recalls a bygone era with its Belter rosewood furniture and marble-topped tables.

Brame-Bennett House
Clinton

A classic example of Greek Revival architecture, Brame-Bennett House was built in 1840 by David Davis, a physician and planter. The house changed hands a number of times until 1887 when the Brame family came into possession.

Letitia Brame, daughter of Judge Franklin Brame, married William H. Bennett. Since then, the house has been owned by the Brame-Bennett families for five generations.

Exquisite antiques, collected throughout the years, fill the interior of the home.

Six Doric columns support the elaborately carved entablature. The pediment contains an unusual sliding fan-shaped window. Another interesting feature of the exterior is the ornamentation above the doorways and windows.

In 1941 the house was the only residence in East Feliciana Parish chosen for a permanent graphic record in the Library of Congress by the Historic American Buildings Survey. The National Register of Historic Places in 1970 added Brame-Bennett House to its list.

This lovely home is presently owned and lived in by Mrs. William Thomas Bennett.

The bright and cheerful parlor in Brame-Bennett House has an Empire sofa and Victorian chairs. Above the mantel hangs a beveled mirror.

A massive mahogany dining table dominates this room at Brame-Bennett House. Note the recessed cabinet filled with old china, figurines, and books.

An unusual curved mantel in a bedroom of the Brame-Bennett House.

An exquisitely carved antique bed, with full tester, seems to invite one to rest awhile at Brame-Bennett House. Against the wall stands a mirrored armoire.

Over eighty years old, this Mallard bed at Brame-Bennett House has a "fainting bench" at its foot. Atop the Empire chest of drawers is a Korean Celadon vase.

Of the Greek Revival style of architecture, Brame-Bennett House's unique underground cistern is unusual. Rainwater was gathered in gutters around the main house and piped into the cistern below ground level. It is reputed to be the only one in existence.

23

Catalpa
St. Francisville

After a fire destroyed the original home on the site, William J. Fort and his wife, Sally Bowman Fort, built Catalpa in 1835. Sally was the daughter of Sarah Turnbull of Rosedown and James Pirrie Bowman of Oakley.

Much of Catalpa's furnishings were originally made or purchased for the elaborate Rosedown mansion.

Moss-draped oaks at Catalpa surround the oldest original slave cabin in Louisiana.

Exquisite miniatures of Turnbull and Bowman's ancestors, a copy of John James Audubon's portrait of Eliza Pirrie, beautiful antiques, china, porcelain, and silver are found in the house.

Wide, brick steps lead to the front gallery, which is encircled by a wooden railing. Six slender colonnettes support a hipped roof. An unusual double-dormer window adds charm to Catalpa's exterior.

Live oak trees, planted as early as 1814, surround the quaint, Victorian cottage. A profusion of shrubs and flowers adds to the beauty of the gardens. Many parties were held on an island in the center of a picturesque pond. It was in this pond that many priceless treasures were hidden during the Civil War.

The strong sense of continuity and reverence for the past at Catalpa is rarely equaled, for the home remains to this day lived in and loved by descendants of the same family.

Prudent Mallard made the dining room furniture at Catalpa. On the mantel are Baccarat crystal candelabras. Fresh flowers add to the room's quiet beauty.

This view of Catalpa's dining room shows the heavy mahogany table, built about 1840. In the corner is a petticoat table with a marble top. Against the wall stands a mahogany etagere.

Prudent Mallard, the distinguished cabinetmaker, fashioned this elegant rosewood parlor set at Catalpa. Delicate French bisque figurines stand on the carved mantelpiece under a painting of an ancestor. An antique beveled mirror hangs above a table made of gold leaf on wood. The tabletop is inlaid with mother-of-pearl.

An antique chest sits in front of the Mallard rosewood bed at Catalpa.

The baby carriage, next to the gentlemen's armoire, is reputed to be the first in the South. An Old Paris washbowl and pitcher on the washstand fascinate the visitor to Catalpa.

Centenary College
Jackson

Towering trees stand guard on the tranquil grounds of Centenary College. Originally opened in 1826 as the College of Louisiana, the school occupied old buildings in the town of Jackson until two dormitories were built on the present property, the east wing in 1832 and the west wing in 1837.

This former professor's home on the Centenary campus is now a visitors' welcome area.

Because of the declining enrollment, the College of Louisiana closed after less than twenty years. It was then merged with Centenary College of Brandon Springs, Mississippi, and was renamed Centenary College of Louisiana. The main academic building was constructed between the two dormitories.

The Civil War had a profound effect on Centenary College. The institution closed for the duration of the war, and its buildings were used alternately by the Confederate and Union troops. The dormitories served as a hospital during the siege of Port Hudson in 1863, and Union troops used the main academic building as headquarters.

The college reopened after the war, but with needed repairs and low enrollment, it was unable to regain its former prosperity. In 1908, seeking a wider student population base, it was moved to Shreveport where it remains today. The main academic building and the east wing were demolished in the 1930s, and only the west wing and a professor's house still stand.

In 1979 the Centenary State Commemorative Area was added to the National Register of Historic Places.

Clinton Courthouse
Clinton

Clinton Courthouse, one of the architectural treasures of Louisiana, was constructed in 1840 and is still in daily use. The present building replaced a wooden courthouse built in 1825 and destroyed by fire just four years later.

Clinton Lawyers' Row
Clinton

Constructed ca. 1840–65, this is an outstanding group of early-nine-teenth-century classical-style offices. Early occupants were noted for their contributions to the political and judicial history of the area and the state.

The Cottage
St. Francisville

On a high bluff in the rolling hills near St. Francisville, the Cottage was built in 1795 by John Allen and Patrick Holland on land granted to them by Spain. The architecture and furnishings clearly indicate Spanish as well as English influence. Purchased in 1811 by Judge Thomas Butler, a well-known jurist and planter, the home was occupied and preserved by the Butler family for the century and a half before J. E. Brown bought it in 1951.

The Cottage had its most famous visitor in 1815 when Gen. Andrew Jackson and his staff stayed there en route north after the Battle of New Orleans.

Beautiful antiques, mostly in Queen Anne style, fill the interior of the house, which differs from later plantation homes. It obviously was intended to be the hub of activity on a working plantation. Many old buildings remain today: the judge's law office, the kitchen, the milk house, the saddle room, and the stable.

Slender columns span the front gallery and support a high-pitched, gabled roof. The enclosed staircase was originally built outside of the house because indoor stairways were heavily taxed by the Spanish crown.

A productive plantation for nearly two hundred years, the Cottage today is owned and operated by the heirs of Mr. and Mrs. J. E. Brown of Glencoe, Illinois.

The furniture in the parlor at the Cottage dates from 1836. Made by Hoadley, the Sheraton-style grandfather clock was crafted from cherry wood and inlaid with contrasting woods. The antique etagere displays old china on its shelves.

Against this parlor window at the Cottage stands an old organ with foot pedals.

An ornate, oval mirror hangs above the black Adams mantelpiece, which is flanked by a china cabinet and an etagere. The old-fashioned wallpaper lends charm to the dining room at the Cottage.

At the northeast end of the Cottage is the bedroom that had been used by Miss Louise Butler, the last member of the Butler family to occupy the house. The antique canopied bed has a prayer bench in front of it and a pot de chambre on the side. Old dolls and children's toys add to the atmosphere of the room.

The square piano at Ellerslie, no longer playable.

Ellerslie
Near Bains

On a high bluff in the Tunica hills, Judge William C. Wade built Ellerslie in 1835. He had come to the Felicianas from the Carolinas in 1830 and had married Olivia Ruffin Lane, a granddaughter of the remarkable pioneer, Olivia Ruffin Barrow.

Following Judge Wade's ownership, the splendid home was occupied by the Percy family, relatives of the Percy daughters who attended Beech Wood school, at which Lucy Bakewell Audubon, wife of noted naturalist John James Audubon, taught for many years.

A gracefully curving mahogany staircase, seemingly unsupported, rises from the hall to the upper levels. Both lower and upper floors feature a wide hall in the center with large rooms on either side.

Ellerslie ranks as one of the most nearly perfect examples of Greek Revival construction. Massive, plastered-brick Doric columns support the heavy entablature. Wide galleries and a glass-enclosed observatory add to the beauty of the exterior.

Owned by descendants of Edward Percy, Ellerslie today stands elegantly beneath age-old oaks. It presents a breathtaking view in spring when the azalea and camellia plants are in bloom, while the mighty oaks, draped in Spanish moss, give the feeling that one has returned to a bygone era.

An old trunk in front of the full-tester rosewood bed at Ellerslie.

Heavy cane-backed chairs surround this antique walnut table at Ellerslie. A carved sideboard, holding an old china tea set, adds to the charm of this comfortable dining room.

In the upstairs hallway at Ellerslie is this antique bookcase with pierced carving on top.

Elaborate detail of Glencoe's second-floor gallery.

Glencoe

Near Jackson

When the original Glencoe was built in 1870, it was the home of Robert Emerson Thompson and his wife, Martha Emily Scott Thompson. Martha had inherited the property from her father, Gustavus Adolphus Scott, who had purchased the land and named it Glencoe after his grandfather's hometown in Scotland.

Robert and Martha Thompson had six daughters and one son. In 1898 the family attended a party at nearby Oakland plantation in Gurley. Upon returning they found their beautiful home, which had been shingled with cedar shakes, destroyed by fire. Thompson turned to his weeping wife and said, "Don't cry, Millie. I'll build another one, but this time I'll shingle it with silver dollars." That explains the silver shingles, made of galvanized aluminum, on the present Glencoe, which was completed in 1903.

Until the arrival of the boll weevil, Glencoe was a productive cotton plantation. As his fortunes changed, Thompson decided to raise livestock, and the plantation became a cattle ranch. It is said that he was the first person in

America to import an entire herd of Brahman cattle. Thirty-two were purchased in India by Thompson, but only eight survived the quarantine in New York City. Mr. and Mrs. Warren J. Westerfield of New Orleans bought the property in 1961 from Robert Emerson Thompson, Jr., and his wife, Azile Edwards Thompson.

Described as the finest example of Victorian-Gothic architecture in Louisiana, Glencoe was listed in the National Register of Historic Places in 1980.

Through the archway of the bedroom at Glencoe one can see into the adjoining sitting room, which is located in one of the Victorian turrets.

Victorian furniture and carved-cypress mantelpiece in the parlor at Glencoe.

Greenwood

Near St. Francisville

Built in 1830 by William Ruffin Barrow and his wife, Olivia Ruffin Barrow, Greenwood plantation home was destroyed by fire in 1960. The twenty-eight plastered-brick columns, broken fireplaces, and a mass of smoldering ashes were all that remained of the grand Greek Revival mansion.

In April of 1968, Walton J. Barnes, father of the present owner, purchased the property and determined to restore Greenwood to its former glory. Photographs of the original home were used to provide detail for rebuilding the moldings, gallery railings, and decor. A fascinating old inventory book describing the interior furnishings for each room was found and helped guide the restoration.

The location of load-bearing walls, the ceiling heights, and the floor dimensions were determined from the ruins by Michael Rollinger, who drew the blueprints for the replica of the historic plantation home.

During the summer of 1968 the Barnes family cleared the site of trees, vines, and weeds. Through the winter of 1968 and into the spring of 1969, Richard Barnes continued the process of site preparation, including the task of digging out and hauling away nearly three feet of ashes and hundreds of pounds of brickwork from the ruined chimneys.

In the following years the actual restoration took place. Each of the twenty-eight columns was restored, using the original bricks, and each was given a

new concrete foundation. The Barneses further improved the grounds by trimming stately oaks and landscaping the gardens. Before proceeding to the building of the mansion, the access roads also were graded.

By 1983 Greenwood had been restored to its former grandeur. The same year International Cinema Corporation contracted to use the plantation as the setting for the film *Louisiana*. Thus, with dedication, hard work, and the assistance of family, friends, and the movie industry, Richard Barnes and his family have realized a dream. Once again, Greenwood is a magnificent Greek Revival plantation home.

This elegant, curving stairway graces the hallway at Greenwood. The magnificent archway, with a pilaster and a column on each side, the delicate antique furniture, and the soothing pattern of the wallpaper enhance a feeling of serenity.

Greenwood's walnut dining room table and chairs date from 1885 and are part of the Barnes family collection from Welham Plantation, the childhood home of Richard Barnes.

Above the mantelpiece in the ladies' parlor at Greenwood hangs a beveled French mirror. An antique rug adds to the quiet beauty of the room. Through the archway the dining room seems to invite entry.

On the east wall of the gentlemen's parlor at Greenwood, the portraits of William Ruffin Barrow and his wife, Olivia Ruffin Barrow, are displayed.

An 1850 Fischer square grand piano dominates the music room at Greenwood. Music was an integral part of plantation entertainment.

Highland

North of Bains

A winding road, lined with lush shrubbery, colorful flowers, and century-old oak trees, leads to Highland plantation house, built by William Barrow III in 1804 on a land grant from the Spanish crown.

The home was originally called Locust Ridge and was later renamed by Barrow's son, Bennett, who introduced to the area a long staple cotton which he called "Highland." After his father's death, Bennett H. Barrow enlarged the house and planted eighty-nine live oak trees during the 1830s. He also added a race track and a sugar mill. A dance hall and a hospital were built for his slaves. His diary, a fascinating commentary on life at Highland from 1836 to 1846, reflects the planter's life and views.

Mr. and Mrs. J. Barrow Norwood, the present owners, restored the house in 1960. At the time of the restoration some of the basic timbers showed deterioration. To make the necessary replacements, Norwood tore down what was left of the old slave cabins, which were built of virgin cypress, to use in the restoration process. The handmade bricks used in the foundation, where replacements were necessary, came from the slave cabin chimneys and the racing stables which were located near the house.

J. Barrow Norwood is the great-great-grandson of the original builder. Six generations of the same family have occupied the home.

Highland has been placed on the National Register of Historic Places.

The Hepplewhite table in Highland's entrance hallway dates from the late 1700s.

A closeup view of the magnificent full-tester bed made in 1854 for Highland.

Portraits of Bennett H. Barrow and his wife Emily Barrow hang above the carved-cypress mantelpiece in the parlor at Highland.

Lakeview
Ethel

In the early 1800s many Americans from the eastern seaboard states began to settle in Louisiana. William East and his parents came to East Feliciana Parish from South Carolina in 1811. Lakeview was built by East about 1830.

Hand-carved wainscoting, paneling covering the lower three or four feet of an interior wall, is found throughout this home. Many windows still contain original hand-

American Federal period secretary in the parlor at Lakeview.

blown panes of glass. Magnificent antiques create an elegant atmosphere.

Lakeview was constructed of heart of pine in the Carolina I architectural style. The gallery, which extends across the center portion of the house, seems made for rocking in the cool evening breezes. Slender, square columns support the slanted roof. Wooden railings enclose the gallery and the wide stairway leading to it.

Beautifully restored by its previous owners, Dr. and Mrs. Kernan Irwin, Lakeview is now lovingly maintained by its present owners, Martha and J. William Carr.

Above the mantelpiece in the parlor at Lakeview is a portrait of Richard Flower, an ancestor, who was married in 1843 to Minerva Scott, daughter of Judge Thomas Scott, of Oakland.

Mahogany table and chairs in the Queen Anne style dominate the dining room at Lakeview. A stately pier mirror, ca. 1875, stands against the wall.

Lane Plantation Home
Near Clinton

Amid sylvan, tranquil surroundings, Lane Plantation Home stands with dignity. It was built between 1825 and 1830 by William A. Lane, who had moved to Louisiana from Maine.

The interior of the house has many interesting original pieces of furniture that were crafted on the plantation. Original panes of glass remain in many of the windows. Heart of pine was used in the construction of the lovely old home, which is in the Carolina I style. When complete restoration took place in 1969, a kitchen wing and a master bedroom were added.

Lane Plantation Home has remained in the same line of ownership throughout the years. The caretaker, Christine Johnson, is a descendant of one of the plantation's original workers.

Andrew Lane Plauché, son of Cornelia Lane, is the present owner. A well-known attorney in Lake Charles, he and his family visit the comfortable plantation home on weekends and vacations.

The bright, cheerful dining room at Lane has several pieces of furniture original to the house: the chairs around the table, the small high chair, the china cabinet, and the old trunk in the corner.

To the side of the massive old sofa at Lane Plantation Home is this antique marble-topped table.

In the second-story hallway at Lane stands this antique sewing machine.

Live Oak
Near Bains

Part of a 1796 Spanish land grant, Live Oak changed hands about fifteen times prior to 1928. In July of 1800 the land was sold by John O'Conner to Elijah Adams and his brother-in-law. It apparently was Adams who built the house in 1808. After Adams's death in 1816, Bennett Barrow of nearby Rosebank purchased the home and its 553 acres in 1824. For the next century it was owned by a succession of Barrow's descendants.

In 1928 Live Oak was bought by the William T. Le Sassier family, who operated a post office on the ground floor of the home. Upstairs, Mrs. Kate Le Sassier presided over a school for children of the area. The house remained in this family until the present owners took possession in 1975.

The magnificent structure has been authentically restored. The house, two full stories and an attic, has walls of brick, measuring one foot thick downstairs but narrowing slightly in the upper walls. Framing timbers are of rough-cut poplar, and much of the fine interior woodwork is also of poplar. Four heavy columns of rounded brick support the upper front gallery. Slender columns support the high-pitched roof. The simple floorplan includes four rooms with no dividing hallways on each story. The floors are connected by a tiny, hidden interior stairway, as well as by the two exterior ones.

During the 1930s a young girl fell in love with a watercolor of the house and purchased it on Royal Street in New Orleans. Throughout the years she grew to feel that the house, which she had seen only in her cherished painting, was somehow destined to be hers one day. In a happy quirk of fate, the young girl and her husband, Sue and Bert Turner of Baton Rouge, now own and cherish the fully restored Live Oak plantation house, which has been added to the National Historic Register.

Above the impressive dining room table at Live Oak hangs this unusual chandelier. The brick-lined mantelpiece stands next to the hidden interior stairway, which leads to the upper floor.

Note the unique chandelier above the game table in the comfortable sitting room at Live Oak.

Locust Grove Cemetery
Near St. Francisville

Without perception of the tragedy that would take place, Luther L. Smith built Locust Grove plantation home on a Spanish land grant in 1806. He was married to Anna Eliza Davis, sister of Jefferson Davis, who later became president of the Confederacy.

Sarah Knox Taylor, daughter of Zachary Taylor, who later became president of the United States, met Jefferson Davis in 1832 at Fort Crawford, Wisconsin. She was eighteen years of age, and he was twenty-six.

Davis was a West Point graduate serving under Colonel Taylor, who stamped his disapproval on the affair. From all accounts, the main objection was Taylor's unwillingness to allow another daughter to submit to the rigors of Army frontier life and the deprivations that it entailed. His oldest daughter, Anne, had married an Army surgeon and had recently given birth in the frontier post located in the wilderness of Minnesota.

Jeff Davis resigned his commission from the Army in 1835 because of the many obstacles to the marriage. Having waited for Knox (as she was called) for three years, he could wait no longer.

Some of the bitterness must have subsided, for Knox was to marry Jefferson Davis, now a plantation owner. Jeff's oldest brother had given him 1,800 acres of land adjoining his plantation near Vicksburg, Mississippi. Jeff and Knox were married at Beechlands, near Louisville, Kentucky, a plantation owned by

The Felicianas

1 Afton Villa Gardens
2 Asphodel
3 Camilla Leake Barrow House
4 Bonnie Burn
5 Brame-Bennett House
6 Catalpa
7 Centenary College
8 Clinton Courthouse
and Lawyers' Row
9 The Cottage
10 Ellerslie
11 Glencoe
12 Greenwood
13 Highland
14 Lakeview
15 Lane Plantation Home
16 Live Oak
17 Locust Grove Cemetery
18 Marston House
19 Milbank
20 The Myrtles
21 Oakland
22 Oakley
23 The Oaks
24 Parlange
25 Propinquity
26 Retreat Plantation House
and St. Mary's Church
27 Richland
28 Rosale
29 Rosebank
30 Rosedown
31 Roseneath
32 The Shades
33 Silliman Institute
34 Stonehenge
35 Wakefield
36 Wall House
37 Wildwood

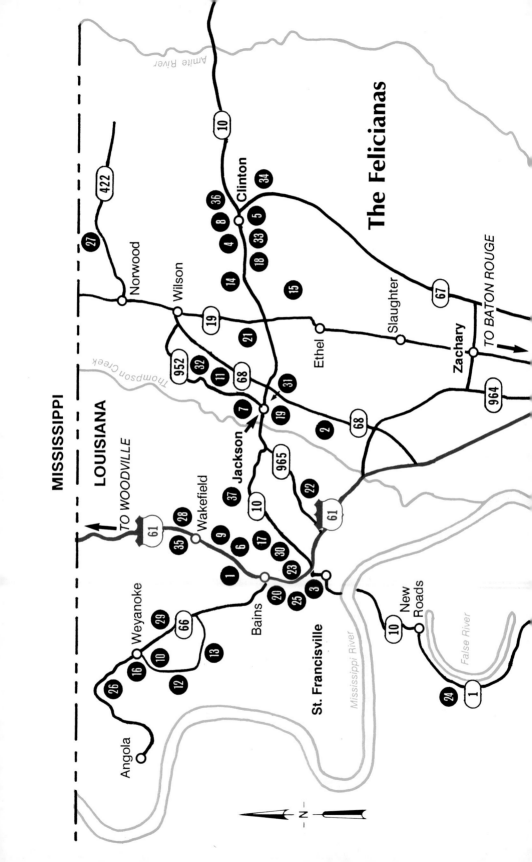

Upstairs view of the hidden stairway at Live Oak.

The splendid full-tester, antique bed dominates this bedroom at Live Oak.

Colonel Taylor's sister, Elizabeth. Most of the family was in attendance and gave their blessings.

The young couple joyfully set forth on the trip down the Mississippi River to their new plantation, which was to be called Brierfield. Fate was not to be kind, however, as the next three months unfolded. Before plantation life had even become routine, she and Jeff were stricken with a fever. Alarmed, Jeff's brother, Joseph, sent them by boat to Locust Grove plantation, the home of Luther and Anna Davis Smith.

As they lay critically ill in separate bedrooms, Jeff heard a song of their courtship days, "Fairy Bells", coming from Knox's room. He struggled to her room and held her in his arms as she died.

His recovery from the illness, her untimely death, and guilt feelings associated with their unsanctioned marriage, took eight years. He retired to Brierfield as a recluse on his plantation until he was thirty-five. Greatness was his destiny, but he remained an austere and melancholy man for the remainder of his life.

The historic Locust Grove plantation home burned in the 1930s and the ruins were later demolished.

Sarah Knox Davis, the charming, witty, mischievous wife of Jefferson Davis, was buried in this crypt.

Marston House
Clinton

Now the headquarters for the East Feliciana Pilgrimage and Garden Club, Marston House was originally built as a bank in 1837.

Spanning the width of the Greek Revival structure are six impressive plastered-brick Ionic columns which support a massive entablature. A palladian window adds to the elegance of the pediment.

This historic building was placed on the National Register of Historic Places in 1971.

Milbank

Jackson

Milbank was built in the 1830s as the banking house for the Clinton/Port Hudson Railroad which traveled through Jackson. The establishment of the bank was instrumental in the growth of the town.

The building's imposing structure has a long, rich history, having housed some fifteen different businesses since its days as a bank. At one time it was the home of the first Jackson newspaper, the *Mirror*. In 1970,

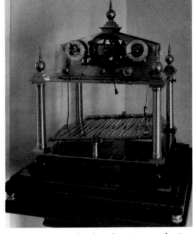

An antique clock of unique design stands on a pedestal in a corner of the Milbank parlor.

the Miller family purchased the building, began a major restoration, and made it their residence. The home has since changed ownership.

Because it was originally built for use as a bank, the interior floor plan differs from most homes of the antebellum period. The hallways, upper and lower, are located on one side of the house, and all the rooms are on the other side. The present owners have chosen to furnish the interior with antiques reflecting the 1800s.

Constructed of solid brick, Milbank's walls are two feet thick. Six impressive, plastered-brick Doric columns, front and rear, support the entablature.

This magnificent home is beautifully maintained by the present owners, Mr. and Mrs. Leroy Harvey of Jackson and Mr. Harvey's sister, Mrs. Thomas Jackson of Bogalusa.

Milbank's formal parlor is sometimes called the music room because of the musical instruments kept here. This view shows an antique square piano and a Spanish music cabinet made of cross-banded kingwood with gold Ormolu mounts on the front panels. The clock on top of the cabinet was made by Boque of Paris. In front of the American Victorian rosewood parlor set stands a black-lacquered opium chest, ca. 1860.

Against the Milbank parlor wall is a Dutch mahogany marquetry secre-taire, dated 1840. It appears to be a chest of drawers, but the second drawer pulls out to convert it into a secretary.

This antique rosewood piano at Milbank was made by Steinway & Son in 1857. The brass plate on the harp is inscribed, "Made by Broderys and Wilkinson in Haymarket, London."

In the dining room at Milbank this spectacular solid-mahogany table commands attention. Surrounding it are unusually wide Irish Chippendale chairs. The silver candelabras were commissioned by Napoleon III in 1855 and bear the Napoleonic "N" and crown on the shields. Made by G. Stomes in Blackburn, England, the grandfather clock has a solid porcelain face.

One of the 80-pound Napoleonic candelabras at Milbank.

Although this room at Milbank is called the French Bedroom, the solid-brass bed is believed to have been owned by King Alphonso of Spain.

Blue window drapes, a blue rug, and blue-tufted satin lining the half-tester contribute to the serene atmosphere of this bedroom at Milbank. The furniture is made of rosewood and walnut.

The mahogany staircase dominates the entrance hallway at the Myrtles.

The Myrtles
St. Francisville

An elegant and mysterious mansion, the Myrtles was built on a Spanish land grant in 1796 by Gen. David Bradford, an exile from what was then the United States. Bradford had been a hero of the American Revolution, but he became involved in the Whiskey Rebellion of 1794 and had to flee to West Feliciana, which was Spanish territory at that time. He died in 1817, and the property passed to a succession of families.

Some of the finest examples of plaster friezework are found throughout the interior of the house. The Baccarat chandelier in the entrance hallway originally burned candles. The two parlors have ornate mirrors at opposite ends, twin Carrara marble mantels, chandeliers, and identical medallions. Wide galleries ornamented with elaborate ironwork grace the exterior of the one-and-a-half-story house. The high-pitched roof is broken by several dormer windows.

There allegedly have been sightings of ghosts at the Myrtles. Strange happenings remain unexplained: an unseen baby cries, the harmonium plays without human assistance, and the specter of a servant, who wore a *tignon* (turban) to hide the loss of an ear, wanders through the house.

The original pieces of art, the antique furnishings, and the beautifully restored house are all carefully maintained by the present owners.

Happy hours are spent in the game room at the Myrtles. Note the antique game table.

This closeup corner view of the parlor at the Myrtles calls attention to the beauty of the unique cornice-work, the Carrara marble mantelpiece, and the Gilbert harmonium.

Against the wall of the dining room at the Myrtles is this early-nineteenth-century chest. The late-eighteenth-century table and chairs are of satinwood.

In a corner of the ground-floor bedroom at the Myrtles stand two chairs with a swan motif. They were designed for Napoleon and Josephine.

The intricately carved medallion in the bedroom at the Myrtles, done in 1840, shows pineapples, grapes, and many different faces. The French beveled mirror above the marble mantelpiece has pierced carving at the top of the ornate frame. Twenty-carat gold trims the Louis XV bed.

Oakland
Gurley

Impressive live oak trees and flowering plants surround Oakland, which was built by Judge Thomas W. Scott who came to Louisiana from South Carolina. The house is approximately 160 years old.

Judge Scott's daughter, Ellen, was married to Iveson Greene Gayden, and for many years the house was known as the Gayden Place. Gayden named the lovely home, however, after Oakland College in Mississippi, which he had attended.

A concealed staircase in the interior of Oakland gives access to the upper floors. Two of the six Adams mantelpieces have a sunburst design, which is repeated in the iron firebacks. An interesting wing leads to Judge Scott's office, where law books line the walls.

A Federal period, three-story house, Oakland reflects the plantation style of South Carolina, with a gallery spanning the front of the lower floor. Heart of pine was used in its construction. Windows, many with the original panes of glass, are above and below the gallery roof. The fifty-eight original blinds are painted dark green with a blackish cast. A two-story brick building to the side of the house contains the original kitchen and dining room where the reception was held when Ellen Scott married Iveson Gayden.

William Hutchinson McClendon III, a young attorney, and his wife, Eugenia Slaughter, bought Oakland in February of 1976. At that time it was in a state of disrepair. The McClendons have restored Oakland to its original magnificence.

The original office of Judge Thomas W. Scott was lined with law books. Today it is lined with law books belonging to William Hutchinson McClendon III, the present owner of Oakland.

This Adams mantelpiece, of unusual Greek Revival design at Oakland, has inlaid bricks around the fireplace and a brass firescreen. Needlepoint tapestry covers the chairs, and the mahogany Empire table is topped with marble.

Each Adams mantelpiece at Oakland is slightly different from the others. A carved sunburst design graces this one in the dining room. Note the simple, but elegant, chandelier above the mahogany table.

To the side of Oakland stands this brick building housing the original kitchen. The old artifacts in the room are eye-catching.

Oakley
St. Francisville

This tall, airy house where John James Audubon stayed was built in 1799 by Ruffin Gray, who died before its completion. Lucy Alston, Gray's widow, inherited the Spanish land grant of 700 arpents and, through wise management, added 1,000 acres to the prosperous plantation.

Lucy later married James Pirrie and they had one daughter, Eliza, who became an impetuous young lady. The Pirries engaged Audubon for four months to tutor Eliza, allowing him half of each day to roam the woods, studying and painting birds. During this short period he produced thirty-two of his famous paintings.

The rooms at Oakley have been furnished in the style of the Federal period (1790–1830), duplicating their appearance when Audubon resided there.

The house reflects the expertise of colonials in dealing with a hot and humid climate. The shallow depth, the protective galleries, and the heavy jalousies all reflect the influence of the West Indies method of climate control. Simple and dignified, the building blends into its beautiful forest setting.

In 1973, Oakley was placed on the National Register of Historic Places.

This implement beside the Oakley greenhouse was used for grading walkways.

The large, detached plantation kitchen, typical of the period, was reconstructed at Oakley on the old foundation around the original chimney.

In this Oakley bedroom are a four-poster mahogany bed with a mosquito bar draped over it and a youth bed with a crochet cover on top. The beds are separated by an intricately carved cypress mantelpiece with iron inlay. The vases are ca. 1850.

The full-tester walnut bed in Eliza Pirrie's bedroom at Oakley stands next to the carved mantelpiece. An Audubon print, Pine Creeping Warbler, adds elegance to the room.

The plantation barn at Oakley displays numerous field tools and implements used to till the soil.

The Oaks

St. Francisville

Surrounded by plantings of old-fashioned flowering trees and shrubs, the Oaks plantation home stands at the end of an entrance roadway lined by century-old oak trees. It was built in 1888 by Judge Thomas Butler on a tract of land that was originally part of Rosedown. Judge Butler, a Civil War veteran, came from a distinguished West Feliciana family. His grandfather, also a judge, settled at the Cottage in 1811. His great-grandfather, born in Ireland, came to the United States in 1748 and was one of the "Five Fighting Butlers" of Revolutionary War fame. The five brothers were commended for gallantry by George Washington and Lafayette, and one of the Butlers first planted the American flag on the British works at Yorktown after General Cornwallis surrendered.

The house was built in a style now termed Carpenter Gothic in tribute to the powered saws and turning lathes of the late 1800s. It abounds in the exuberance of gingerbread, dormer windows, and fanciful turrets now deemed worthy of the preservationist's notice.

Constructed of pine and cypress, with fourteen-foot ceilings, plastered walls, heart-of-pine flooring, and fine interior wainscoting and moldings, the house has a central hallway which is entered through double entrance doors.

When the last member of Thomas Butler's family died in 1973, the still-prosperous and productive plantation was purchased by E. Irwin Daniel III, whose family delights in its romantic atmosphere.

The Oaks is listed in the National Register of Historic Places.

The antique parlor set at the Oaks is accented by a gilt-framed pier mirror, equal in height to the eleven-foot windows.

The dining room at the Oaks features a bay window with colorfully hued panes and a crystal chandelier dating from the 1800s.

Parlange
Near New Roads

One of the oldest plantation homes in Louisiana, Parlange was built in 1750 under the direction of Marquis Vincent de Ternant on a land grant from the French crown. His son, Claude Vincent, inherited the plantation upon his father's death in 1757.

After his first wife's death, Claude married Virginie Trahan, his young cousin and ward. Her forceful, vibrant personality contributed great-

Two identical pigeonniers flank Parlange Plantation House.

ly to the success of his prosperous plantation. The couple had five children, two of whom died in early childhood. Of the three remaining children, the older daughter, Marie Virginie, was reared and educated in Paris where she married and lived the rest of her life. The son died in early manhood. The delicate, frail younger daughter, Julie, died on her wedding night and was buried the next day in her bridal gown.

Virginie married Col. Charles Parlange, an officer in the French army, several years after the death of her first husband. Charles, Jr., was their only child.

During the Civil War, Parlange alternately served as Union headquarters for Gen. Nathaniel Banks and as Confederate headquarters for Gen. Dick Taylor. Though the beautiful home was not destroyed by the Union forces, it did suffer from the ravages of war.

After the war Charles, Jr., restored the plantation to its original state. He later studied law and became a noted attorney. He was elected Louisiana state senator, United States district attorney, lieutenant governor of Louisiana, federal judge, and justice of the Louisiana Supreme Court.

When Charles's son, Walter Charles Parlange, also a noted attorney, married Paule Brierre of an old New Orleans family, he gave up his legal career and brought his bride home to Parlange. Restoration once again took place.

The design of Parlange is similar to that of French plantation homes in the West Indies. It is constructed of cypress and bricks, which were prepared on the plantation site. The walls are made of *bousillage*, a mixture of mud, moss, and deer hair. Galleries surround the structure. In the dormer windows, tiny panes of glass, eighteen over eighteen, clearly indicate that this is a very early home.

Walter C. Parlange, Jr., and his vivacious wife, Lucy Brandon Parlange, own and operate their vast plantation, which is still prosperous and productive. They have three children: Walter III, Brandon, and Angele.

Parlange is a National Historic Landmark.

In an elaborate gold-leaf frame, a magnificent portrait of Madame Virginie de Ternant Parlange hangs on the wall of the salon at Parlange. It was painted by Dubufe, artist in the court of Emperor Napoleon III, and his wife, Eugenie.

In keeping with the Henry Clay bedroom furniture, the armoire is massive and intricately carved.

The gigantic Henry Clay bed at Rosedown.

In 1844 Henry Clay announced his candidacy for the office of president of the United States. A few of his friends engaged a Philadelphia firm of cabinetmakers to create a great Gothic bedroom suite for Clay to use in the White House. When he lost the election, his friends put the furniture up for sale. Daniel Turnbull then bought it for Rosedown.

While in Paris, Martha and Daniel Turnbull purchased this scenic wallpaper for Rosedown. Designed by Joseph Dufour, a celebrated craftsman, it enhances the breathtaking foyer.

The Carrara marble mantelpiece dominated the parlor at Rosedown. The hand-and-arm tiebacks holding the window draperies are unique.

The original furnishings purchased by the Turnbulls for Rosedown included this Regency mahogany dining table, Phyfe chairs, and a French Empire serving table with console marble top. On one side of the cotton covering of the punkah are flowers and cotton blossoms.

Rosedown

St. Francisville

Daniel Turnbull, a wealthy planter, made an entry in his journal on November 3, 1834, which signaled the beginning of work to create Rosedown. Construction of the home was completed in 1835.

He and his wife, Martha Barrow Turnbull, shortly before had returned from their wedding trip to Europe where they had purchased magnificent furnishings for the mansion they intended to build. At Versailles and in the gardens of Italy Martha saw avenues of trees, statuary, formal parterres, and garden ornaments in the French style of the seventeenth century. Plans for her garden began to form in her mind, and on her return her plans were carried out.

Today the interior of Rosedown is filled with beautiful antiques, reflecting the elegant lifestyle of the antebellum years.

Impressive Doric columns extend across the two-story central section of the house. Wooden balustrades of classic design encircle both upper and lower galleries. Cypress and cedar used in building this spectacular mansion came from a swamp woodland on the property and was processed at the plantation's sawmill. One-story plastered-brick wings, each with a portico and columns, were built on either side of the house.

Descendants of the Turnbulls lived in the home until 1956 when the late Catherine Fondren Underwood of Houston, Texas, bought and restored Rosedown to its original grandeur.

The dining room at Rosebank, with original brick flooring.

Rosebank

Near Bains

While the exact date of construction is unknown, Rosebank exhibits definite evidence of early Spanish influence, particularly in its exterior staircases and the straight, unbroken line of its cedar-shake roof. The land was part of a 1790s Spanish land grant held by an Irishman, John O'Conner, who served as *alcade* of the district during the last years of Spanish rule. O'Conner is said to have operated an inn on the lower floor of the house.

In 1818 the house was purchased by Bennett Barrow, brother of Bartholomew Barrow of Afton Villa. Bennett Barrow became a cotton planter and political leader, representing the parish in the Louisiana Legislature in 1827.

Bennett's youngest son, Robert James Barrow, who had been only seven months of age when the family came to Louisiana, inherited Rosebank at age sixteen. It was Robert's wife who gave Rosebank its name and planted the profusion of old-fashioned bulbs which brighten its lawn in early spring with colorful blooms.

Misfortune plagued Robert Barrow's life. His first four children died in infancy, and he suffered numerous financial setbacks. The Civil War brought still another reversal when he was taken prisoner by Union soldiers.

The lower floor has eighteen-inch-thick walls of *bousillage*, a mixture of mud, moss, and deer hair. The bricks used in the exterior walls and the flooring of the ground level were made on the plantation. The upper levels contain the main living quarters and are solidly constructed of cypress and blue poplar. Wooden pegs join the mortised beams and joists. Four Doric columns support the upper-floor gallery, and slender iron colonnettes support the roof.

Restoration has been completed by the present owners.

At the top of the stairway at Rosale was a schoolroom flanked by bed-rooms used by the tutors. This is a closeup view of an original desk.

This view of the original stairway at Rosale shows the attractive design of the rails.

One finds peace and quiet in the serene atmosphere of the gallery at Rosale.

Richland

Norwood

One of the most splendid homes in the Felicianas, Richland was built in 1820 by Elias Norwood for his bride, Katherine Chandler of South Carolina.

Typical of plantation homes built at that time, a wide central hall with rooms on each side runs the length of the house. Elaborate gold-leaf mirrors, crystal chandeliers, and antique furniture fill the interior. Twin fireplaces, one at each end of the double parlor, add an element of cheerful, welcoming warmth. A spectacular winding stairway gives access to the upper levels of the house. The second story has a floor plan similar to that of the first. The third floor, a ballroom in antebellum years, has been converted into bedrooms.

Construction was done by plantation slaves who baked the bricks and cut the timber. Four immense Doric columns span the central section of the façade, supporting wide galleries and a massive entablature. A beautifully designed Palladian window is located near the rooftop on each side of the magnificent structure. The dormered roof and the lower gallery floor are both made of imported slate.

The present owners take delight in maintaining this historic, stately mansion.

Note the elegantly carved woodwork and the exquisite Baccarat crystal chandelier in the cheerful double parlor at Richland.

This magnificent winding staircase graces the hallway at Richland.

Rosale
St. Francisville

West Feliciana Parish is often spoken of as English Louisiana, partially due to the background of the early settlers and partially due to the topography. One will find no better example of that characterization than Rosale.

Surrounded by over 100 magnificent live oak trees, the house is situated on a hill. Rolling hills and heavy forests in the distance give Rosale the appearance of being in the center of an English park.

This chandelier at Rosale once belonged to Gen. William Tecumseh Sherman.

On part of a large Spanish land grant made in 1795 to Alexander Stirling, his daughter Ann and her husband Andrew Skillman built a handsome red brick house in 1836. It had six columns front and back, two-and-a-half stories, and a full basement. A number of additional buildings were constructed near the manor. Two of these are still standing. One, a large two-story plantation schoolhouse, is incorporated in the present house. The other, a large and attractive Greek Revival summerhouse, stands nearby.

In 1845 Ann Skillman sold the plantation, then known as China Lodge, to Robert Hilliard Barrow, Jr., a descendant of the Pirries of Oakley and the Barrows of Highland. Robert and his wife, Mary Eliza, changed the name from China Lodge to Rosale. They lavished attention and money on Rosale, creating

a grand manor and an elegant lifestyle. At that time members of the Barrow clan owned Highland, Greenwood, Rosebank, Live Oak, and Rosedown.

At the onset of the Civil War, Barrow raised and outfitted a company of volunteers, the Rosale Guards. In time he became commander of the Eleventh Louisiana Infantry and commanded that unit at the Battle of Shiloh.

The Civil War and Reconstruction brought an end to the golden era of the planter class. Most of the great houses survived, although ownership changed often, as did the lifestyles of the occupants.

Throughout the years, fire was a constant threat to plantation homes. Indeed, Rosale burned to the ground in 1888. The 1835 two-story school-house, complete with two chimneys, thick plaster walls, heart-of-pine floor-ing, and huge poplar sills, was moved to the site of the original house. To this intact core was added a broader center hallway and several additional rooms, plus a surrounding gallery.

The present owners of Rosale, Gen. and Mrs. Robert H. Barrow, restored the lovely old home in 1984 and 1985.

General Barrow, of the fifth generation bearing the same name, served forty-one years in the United States Marine Corps, retiring as its twenty-seventh commandant in 1983.

A walnut bed, which belonged to General Barrow's great-grandmother, and a youth bed with half-tester, ca. 1870, at Rosale.

Retreat Plantation House
Near Bains

St. Mary's Church, on the grounds of Retreat Plantation.

Retreat Plantation House was built in the early 1850s by Capt. Clarence Mulford on a bluff overlooking Bayou Sara. The timeworn home stands amid old moss-draped oak trees. Cypress and bricks prepared on the plantation were used in its construction. Four stuccoed brick Doric columns span the front of the house and support the steep hipped roof, which is broken by dormer windows.

Retreat is presently owned by Mr. and Mrs. Jim Salvant.

Nearby, in a dense woodland on the grounds of Retreat Plantation, stands St. Mary's Church, alone and neglected. The quaint, Gothic-style church features crenellated tower parapets, lancet windows, and buttresses. An architectural treasure, it is listed on the National Register of Historic Places.

Note the extension of this impressive antique dining table and the singular design of the crystal chandelier in the dining room at Propinquity.

Under this impressive full-tester bed at Propinquity is a trundle bed partially pulled out.

Propinquity
St. Francisville

A trading post was established in 1790 by John Mills in the bustling town of Bayou Sara on the Mississippi River. He chose this location because the river traffic made the landing place lively with commerce, but it was to the high ground of nearby St. Francisville that he turned for a homesite. In 1809 Mills bought a lot in the town on historic Royal Street and built his dwelling. He enjoyed the house for a very short time, however, for he died in 1811.

William Center Wade, parish judge of Feliciana, rented the home for a time before purchasing it in 1816. He owned the property for only three years, but nearly a century and a half later it came into the possession of his great-grandson, Theodore H. Martin. Mr. and Mrs. Martin began thoughtful restoration of the interesting structure and named it Propinquity, meaning kinship or close proximity.

Originally, tapering brick walls fronted on the street. A doorway, now bricked up, gave access to an open gallery with exterior stairs. This gallery was enclosed and the wooden one added in 1826. The asymmetrical floor plan is unusual.

Propinquity was included in the National Register of Historic Places in 1973.

The candles in the original crystal-and-bronze chandelier in the salon at Parlange are still lighted on special occasions.

The extended dining table at Parlange is made of solid cherry wood and has Empire-style chairs on either side. The imposing Jacobean chair at the head of the table bears the Parlange crest at the top.

In springtime the gazebo at Rosedown is surrounded by colorful azaleas.

The quiet beauty of the scene from the rear of Rosedown.

Roseneath

Jackson

The building of Roseneath was begun in 1830 by the Nichols family, but before its completion in 1832 it became the property of Robert Perry, a wealthy planter. Ownership changed several times during the following years, with each occupancy contributing to the cultural life of historic Jackson.

Many antiques, original to the house, add to the elegance of the interior. Typical of southern homes of the period, a wide hallway bisects the house on the first two levels with two twenty-foot-square rooms on each side. The third floor consists of a single room, with a stairway leading to the roof where a widow's walk once afforded a panoramic view of the countryside. Judging from the design of the woodwork and the staircase, which gracefully rises from the entrance hallway to the third floor, construction was done by master artisans.

The imposing exterior features four fluted Doric columns supporting an elaborately carved entablature. A unique balcony is suspended between the columns and the facade.

Originally called "the White House," the magnificent home was renamed "Roseneath" after historical Roseneath Plantation in De Soto Parish, the childhood home of Maria Marshall Dudley, mother of the present owners.

Roseneath is the home of Mr. and Mrs. J. Henry Johnston and Mrs. Anthony Acosta.

Wildwood is exquisitely furnished with Empire and Victorian antiques.

A crystal chandelier hangs above the magnificent dining room set at Wildwood.

Wildwood

Near St. Francisville

In 1915 Wildwood, originally called Arrowhead, was built by architect Robert S. Soulé for his brother, Albert Lee Soulé, a highly respected educator from New Orleans. Soulé's father had founded Soulé Commercial College in New Orleans in 1856, and the Feliciana home provided the family needed respite on weekends from the responsibilities of running the institute.

Designed as a showcase of the most progressive ideas of the day, the home featured central heating, closets for each bedroom, an intercom

Bohemian crystal chandelier from the Old Wildwood plantation home in Port Hudson.

system, an electric bell for maid service, tile-lined chimneys, and three bathrooms, excluding the one in the basement for the hired help. A laundry chute was built on the second floor, extending to the basement where washing vats were installed. The house also had a butler's pantry and a solarium.

The elder Soulé took a great interest in the home's lawns and planted many camellias which continue to thrive today. He also supervised the planting of the rows of crepe myrtle trees.

In 1958 the magnificent home was sold to the Conrad P. McVea family, and history seemingly repeated itself. The McVeas were both educators, the husband a longtime associate with the State Department of Education and the wife the first-grade teacher for a generation of school children. The McVeas renamed the home Wildwood after their ancestral property near Port Hudson. The completely restored mansion is maintained beautifully.

Pegged, and with original glass, the walnut Pennsylvania corner cupboard at the Wall House dates from 1840.

A Lincoln desk with original glass, dating from 1860, the walnut secretary at the Wall House is carefully preserved.

The carved-cypress mantelpiece, with inlaid brick, is original to the Wall House.

Wall House
Clinton

A quaint cottage called the Wall House stands on a quiet street in the center of Clinton. The original portion of the house was constructed in the late 1830s by the Reverend Isaac Wall, Sr., a Methodist minister originally from New York. His son, Isaac Wall, Jr., enlarged the home in an 1895 remodeling.

Wall House is a story-and-a-half frame house with Queen Anne Revival and Italianate features. It was originally one room deep and three rooms wide. The age of this part of the house is indicated by its wide floorboards and its pit sawed (or water mill sawed) joists. In the late 1800s a front and a side wing were added. The date of these sections of

Of simple design, the mahogany staircase in the entrance hallway at the Wall House has weathered the years well.

the house is corroborated by the fact that the floorboards are narrow and the joists are circular sawed. The floor plan was reworked at that time to include a central hall. The front parlor received a turret with a faceted conical roof.

Architecturally significant, the Wall House is a landmark in Clinton's heritage of late-nineteenth-century residences. It is presently owned by Mr. and Mrs. Randall Peay, who live in this historic home with their children.

The National Register of Historic Places added the Wall House to its list on May 31, 1984.

Wakefield

Near St. Francisville

On November 3, 1834, Lewis Stirling wrote in his diary, "Mitchell came and brought three hands and began work on my house on Monday evening." Completed two years later, the two-and-a-half-story Greek Revival home was named after Oliver Goldsmith's popular novel, *The Vicar of Wakefield*.

The Stirlings traveled to Philadelphia, New York, and London to buy magnificent furnishings. The interior features heart-of-pine flooring and fourteen-foot-high ceilings. Doorknobs are of silver, and immense sliding doors connect the parlor with the dining room. Wakefield has a broad front gallery with six Doric columns supporting the roof, which is broken by a wide dormer window.

Used as a hospital during the Civil War, the plantation has since been the scene of peaceful agricultural ventures. Sugarcane, corn, potatoes, cattle, and sheep have been raised here.

After the Stirlings died in 1877, their heirs effected a strange and dramatic property settlement. With Solomon-like logic, they divided the house into three parts, and in an engineering feat of staggering complexity removed the upper floors so that two separate houses could be built from them. Both have since burned.

The essential Wakefield remains and is now owned and maintained by Dr. and Mrs. Eugene Berry.

Thought to be the only example of its kind in the South, a latticed wood screen with cornice separates the front hall from the rear hall at Stonehenge. The "petticoat table" has a mirror under the marble top so the ladies could see whether their petticoats showed beneath their skirts. Above the settee hangs a painting dating from the 1600s.

This view of the second parlor at Stonehenge shows the delicate silk covering the Victorian furniture.

The mahogany table and chairs dominate the dining room at Stonehenge. Made by Waterford, the crystal is in the Lismore pattern.

Stonehenge
Clinton

High on a hill in a grove of magnificent old trees, Stonehenge stands in stately splendor. Construction took place in 1837 by Judge Lafayette Saunders, who later built the present Clinton courthouse in 1841. He and his family lived in the home for only a brief time. After his young daughter plunged to her death through an open window on the second floor, the Saunders family abandoned the new mansion.

Shortly after the tragedy, Judge John McVea purchased the property. Upon his death in 1876 the estate was inherited by his daughter, Imogen, and her husband, Col. John Stone. The new owners named the home Stonehenge.

The palatial house has upper and lower galleries which span its width. Six imposing, fluted Doric columns support the upper gallery and exquisite, lacy iron filigree supports the sloping roof. The walls are of brick, twelve inches thick.

The present owner is Elizabeth Toler Piker, the daughter of Dr. C. S. Toler, who acquired Stonehenge in 1950.

Silliman Institute
Clinton

Under the influence and leadership of William Silliman, ten public-spirited citizens of East Feliciana Parish, realizing the value of education for young women, formed a corporation in May 1852 and called it Silliman Female Collegiate Institute. A site for the college was obtained in a suburb of Clinton and construction was begun.

In the first year of operation, 1852–53, ninety-six students enrolled. When the Civil War broke out in 1861, the institute's doors were closed and remained so throughout the conflict. Silliman was used as a hospital for wounded soldiers during the Battle of Clinton.

After the Civil War, most of the corporation stockholders were so impoverished that they transferred their interests to William Silliman, the only one possessing the means, and the courage, to proceed. Silliman then transferred the grounds, buildings, and an endowment fund of twenty thousand dollars to the Louisiana Presbytery, the lower court of the Presbyterian Church. The conditions of the donation were that the Presbytery, through its agents and trustees in perpetual succession, would conduct the institution as a college for young ladies, free from all sectarian tenets and religious dogmas. The buildings at the college remained the same until 1894 when a fifty-by-one-hundred-foot structure was added.

Eighteen immense Doric columns span the façade of the three connected, yet dissimilar, structures. Magnificent oak, beech, and magnolia trees shade the campus.

because of her collection of more than 1,000 bells amassed over the years. They are displayed in the house today.

The rectangular structure consists of two stories. It has a steep, double-pitched roof, the lower level of which is supported by massive Doric columns.

The Shades is now owned by Mr. and Mrs. G. V. Berger, who have two daughters, Scott and Jacqueline. Mrs. Berger is the former Edrye Black of Baton Rouge and is a descendant of Alexander Scott. Thus, the Shades remains in the original family's possession.

Original to the house, a beautiful, beveled pier mirror, with pierced carving on top of the ornate frame, graces the dining room at the Shades. The walnut sideboard is also original to the house.

An ancestor's portrait hangs above the carved-cypress mantelpiece in the parlor at the Shades.

The massive four-poster bed in this bedroom at the Shades is in early Louisiana style.

The Shades

Near Gurley

Built of cypress hewn on the plantation, and hand-fashioned bricks, the Shades plantation house was completed in 1808 by Alexander Scott, who had heard intriguing tales of fortunes being made in the lush region of Louisiana. He had originally settled in Black Mingo, South Carolina, and came to Louisiana with his long rifle, which he affectionately called "Old Black Mingo" in tribute to his former home.

A magnificent Prudent Mallard cabinet houses the bell collection at the Shades.

With Old Black Mingo in the crook of his elbow and his dog at his heels, Alexander roamed the woodlands hunting game for his dinner table while he lived in a cabin and watched the walls of his beautiful new home rise.

After having enjoyed the comfort and peace of the Shades for nearly fifty years, Alexander died in the 1840s. Upon his death, the home was inherited by his son, Maj. E. A. Scott, who with his brother, Capt. Gus Scott, served with distinction in the First Louisiana Cavalry during the Civil War. Family records indicate that the major's son, Alexander Scott II, who had inherited some of his grandfather's mettle, ran away from home at the age of fifteen to join the Confederate forces.

The daughter of Alexander Scott II, Eva Scott, was a jolly, well-loved lady who had been born in one of the upstairs bedrooms in 1877. It was during Miss Eva's residency that the home became known as "the house of bells"

In a corner of the parlor at Roseneath stands an antique mahogany secretary of Gothic design.

This massive, Mallard-type mahogany bed at Roseneath has a full tester. In front of the bed is a mahogany settee of unusual design.

The candlesticks in front of the Cheval mahogany mirror at Roseneath were spikes usually used on the four corners of the bed.

The overall view of the parlor, as seen from the dining room, shows gold-leaf valances and gold-leaf mirrors which are original to Roseneath.

A chandelier of unique design hangs above a magnificent table at Roseneath. The table can be lengthened to seat twenty diners.